My Week

Set One: Book I

My Week
My ESOL Readers: Set One: Book 1
ISBN: 978-1-84231-380-0

Text by Rama Rangan
Edited by Bethan Bligh
Illustrations by Lucy Massey

Text copyright © 2025 Rama Rangan
Illustrations copyright © 2025 Gatehouse Books
All rights reserved

First published and distributed in 2025 by Gatehouse Books
Printed by Short Run Press, Exeter, Devon, UK

British Library Cataloguing-in-Publication Data:
A catalogue record for this book is available from the British Library

No part of this publication may be reproduced in any form or by any means, electronic, mechanical, photocopying, recording or otherwise, without the prior written consent of the publishers.

I am Aisha.

On Monday, I go to the supermarket.

I buy fruit and vegetables.

I also buy bread, milk and other things.

On Tuesday, I come to college.

I learn English at college.

I have many friends in class.

I like my college.

On Wednesday, I go to the park.
I go for a long walk.

I look at the pond
and I feed the ducks and birds.

On Thursday, I visit my friend.
We have lunch together.

Sometimes, we go to the shops.

On Friday, I clean my house.
I get very busy with the housework.

I tidy the rooms
and cook for the weekend.

At the weekend, I spend time with my family.

On Saturday, we go for a walk in the park. We watch TV at home. Sometimes, we go shopping.

On Sunday, I read my book.

I do my homework
and get everything
ready for college.

My life in England is very different to life in my country.

Author

Rama Rangan is an ESOL tutor at Warrington & Vale Royal College. She has been a teacher for more than 15 years. Rama speaks six languages and is learning two more!
Rama was inspired to write these books as a learning aid for her students. She has used specific vocabulary and familiar references to make them relevant and engaging.

Editor

Bethan Bligh is Library Manager at Warrington & Vale Royal College. She champions the benefits of reading and promotes the correlation between reading and literacy.